Rewriting Your Mental Script

8 Mindsets That Defeat Self Sabotage

Khadijah Adams

Sisterhood
Publishing
www.sisterhoodextravaganza.org

For Publishing Information Contact:
SisterhoodPublishing@gmail.com

For Book Sales Contact: info@khadijahadams.com

ISBN: 978-1-7362767-0-9

ACKNOWLEDGEMENT

—————— ◆◇◆ ——————

Special thanks to Philippa Burgess for giving me my first real business plan which has proven very successful, and for encouraging me to write a book.

To my beautiful friend, Susan Hwang, thank you for your support and for making me stretch, I will forever cherish our friendship. I especially thank you for introducing me to the FABULOUS Pat Gillum of Sisterhood Publishing. Pat's guidance throughout this process has been incredible and her support, phenomenal!

To my spiritual sister, Lesley Cordova; thank you so much for your assistance, friendship, and patience while on my journey back to the truth.

To my morning motivational group; Alfredah Bey, Vincent Dunn, Larrette Samuel, Leroy Christie, Ms. T. Smith, and Angela Taylor, thank you all for always showing up; always being supportive and especially for helping me choose my perfect book cover!

DEDICATION

———————— ◆ ◇ ◆ ————————

This book is dedicated to everyone who has a genuine desire to rewrite their mental script (change their mindset). It's not as easy as it sounds but with consistent practice, self-awareness, persistence, and the will to never give up; *YOU* <u>*CAN*</u> *DO IT!*

For my sons,
De'Wayne, De'Wight, Victor, and Carey

TABLE OF CONTENTS

INTRODUCTION

What Is A Mental Script?

Not many people realize this, but your thoughts literally shape who you are as a person. There is a bible verse found in Proverbs 23:7 "As a man thinketh in his heart, so is he...." What you think you become. This couldn't be any truer. After all, your thoughts influence your attitude, your attitude influences your actions, and your actions ultimately shape your life and personality.

The thing is, every person's mind is embedded with a pattern of thoughts or, more accurately, a mental script that they may not even be aware of. This mental script is much like a computer's operating system that functions invisibly in the background but dictates everything that happens in the foreground. You could also say that it is a blueprint for your thoughts, and your mind keeps playing it over and over again.

Your mental script influences your identity, behavior, beliefs, actions, preferences, and other things that help you perceive and deal with the world. In doing so, it molds you and your life. So, it is only clear that you should be aware of the type of script you have and take the steps needed to rewrite it to ensure that you live a happy, successful, and fulfilling life.

Rewriting Your Mental Script

Rewriting your mental script is a time-consuming process. This is because it is a result of countless repetitions of the same patterns of thinking, and, over time, these patterns tend to get concretized. Any change to this structure is bound to take some time and effort. Real effort. Only in extreme cases can the process of rewriting be accelerated, like the death of a loved one, an accident, etc.

It's important that you are mindful of this fact before you get started. It will help you stick to the plan and see it through the end. To that end, let's take a look at the step-by-step process you can take to rewrite your mental script.

1) Identifying The Old Script

The first step to solving any problem is to identify it. And here, the problem is your old script. Since you may not be consciously aware of the type of scripts that are embedded in your mind, you may need to do some soul searching. Think about different scenarios that happen regularly in your life and how you react to them. Think about any limiting beliefs you may have about yourself.

Basically, in this first step, you have to become an observer of your own behavior. Make sure you do so in a non-judgmental manner, though. Otherwise, you may slip into a state of guilt, and that will only hinder the process. In this regard, meditation is perhaps the best way to do some effective introspection without judging yourself.

2) Understand YOUR Why

Sometimes, to challenge the status quo, all you need to ask is why. Seriously, some of the biggest changes in history have happened because people dared to ask why. You can do the same with your patterns of thinking. If you don't feel comfortable being all by yourself at the gym, ask yourself why. If you feel like you are not a morning person, again, ask yourself why.

You will realize that most of the time, the same old patterns that you follow just don't have a valid justification. You just follow them because that's what you have always done. And when this realization hits you, you can finally start bringing about change. It will help beat the mental inertia, and you will be able to move to step 3.

3) Start Chipping Away At The Old Script

You can't just get rid of a bad habit and call it a day. In all likelihood, you will return to that old habit eventually. For instance, you can't just quit smoking. You need to replace it with a good habit, at least initially. Similarly, to change old patterns of thinking, you need to replace them with new ones.

Saying positive affirmations will help immensely in this regard. If you didn't already know, it is a powerful practice where you repeat positive statements to yourself. Over time, these statements reprogram your subconscious mind and play an instrumental role in rewriting your mental script. So, instead of thinking that you are not good enough, you may start repeating to yourself that you are an amazing person, that you are very talented, or that you can do anything you put your mind to.

4) Just Stick To It!

In most pursuits in life, success is achieved not by doing something extraordinary but by doing the ordinary without giving up. The same applies here too. It is one thing to realize how your mental scripts are shaping your life and that you need to change them. And it's completely another to keep rewriting these scripts to live life the way you see fit.

If, at any point, you find it hard to fight the old patterns, remind yourself why you are doing this in the first place. If you find it hard to instill a new habit, push through, and remind yourself what this will enable you to do moving forward and into the future. Just stick to it. It will be well worth it in the end.

Forming New Habits That Lead To Success

Rewriting your mental script is a conscious process where you flush out old, useless, limiting, and negative patterns of thoughts and replace them with ones that can enrich your life in various ways. In doing so, you essentially remove the roadblocks that were preventing good habits from entering your life. Since you are in conscious control of the rewriting process, you would obviously choose the new habits carefully. Slowly but surely, these new habits will pave a path to success for you. You will merely have to walk the path that's been laid out in front of you. In the end, you will realize that the mind really is everything. And what you think, you become.

Success is a habit achieved when you have the right mindset. When you force new patterns or routines into your life while still hanging on to your old way of thinking, the new habits will never become effective.

We've all heard that successful people have a daily method of operations, i.e., a daily routine. They do certain things consistently all the time, which is why they achieve a greater degree of success than most other people. However, there's more to it than just that. You've got to do more than do certain things repeatedly to have consistent victory. It's about changing the way you think.

When you implement success habits without changing the way you think (rewriting your mental script), you eventually end up back at square one. Why is this? Because you tried to implement these changes on a shaky psychological foundation. We all know what happens when you build on a shaky foundation. It eventually falls apart.

You have to implement these changes on the right mental foundation at the start so they can become effective. Your mindset is a combination of your beliefs, expectations, and definitions (how you see things). One of the things that successful people have in common is that they share a range of mindsets that empowers them to maintain their success habits. In most cases, they scale them up over time.

A success mindset is not something that you're born with, and it's not something that you have, or you don't. If you ask successful people how they developed their mindsets, many will confess that their winning attitude was created and cultivated through trial and error and plain ole life lessons.

It's a good thing that you don't have to go through those headaches, heartbreaks, and frustrations if you haven't already. This book is your head start into identifying and implementing new mindsets that can eventually lead you to consistent victory, over and over again.

This book will give you different perspectives on how to rewrite your mental script. Since you can't go back and change your past, it suggests habits that can help you start implementing key mindsets that lead to success. Each philosophy has a division of beliefs. Let's review them together and discuss how you can start implementing them into your life to change your results.

How Important Are Beliefs?

When you change your mindset, you rewrite your mental script, thereby changing your system of beliefs. Without rewriting your mental script, you'll project thoughts that won't help you on your journey to success. In many cases, limiting beliefs hold you back and keep you from the success that you could have otherwise achieved.

You must rewrite your mental script so that it leads you to the right set of beliefs. These beliefs shape the way you respond to everything that happens to you directly; they shape what's going on around you, your priorities, your core values, and they even shape the direction of your life. That's how important beliefs are.

On the flip side, you are in control of what you believe, and you can always change your beliefs if you want to, and with consistent practice. If you believe that some people have it all, it's because you think they've made the right choices. In this book, I'm going to walk you through clearing your mind of toxic beliefs so you can rewrite your mental script by identifying and adopting the right mindset that helps lead you to achieve more significant results.

Let's start by laying a solid mental foundation that allows you to create and implement the right success habits that leads to consistent victory in almost every aspect of your life.

Chapter One

GETTING RID OF MENTAL BLOCKS

Okay, so let's be clear. I know you're excited about rewriting your mental script so you can "Boss Up". Kinda like the Beyonce song, "Upgrade You", you acquired this book because you are actively looking to achieve greater success by upgrading your lifestyle. You want better results, I get it. However, the real issue is, you're holding on to a "toxic" mindset (belief system) that actually sets you up for failure and ultimately you end up sabotaging yourself. Ask me how I know. Yup, that part. I've been there and done that. I even got a trophy.

To start this process, you must first clear mental roadblocks *(commonly known as 'toxins')* from your mind before you start implementing positive mindsets. Otherwise, those toxins will keep weighing you down, negatively affecting you, and in most cases, you'll end up never achieving any real success. Get rid of the mental roadblocks that's holding you back. Doing so puts you in the position to achieve the success you desire.

Mental Roadblock #1: Playing the Blame Game

First off, you should know that amateurs blame others for their disappointments and failures, but professionals don't. Professionals take responsibility for their failures and view them as either lessons learned, or blessings earned. Successful people admit when they've messed up. Then, they take the necessary steps to learn what is required to help them implement new ways to turn their failures into successes.

One of the most popular games people play with themselves is thinking their setbacks is the responsibility of "other people". Maybe these "other people" were sabotaging them, or maybe they were just negligent. Whatever your reasoning is, if you have this toxic mindset, you believe the reason you're failing is because of "other people". What's even worse, this also applies to situations beyond your control. Being in that position is often comforting for many people. Settling into this way of thinking reduces them into victims. Victims often seek out sympathy because most people have a natural tendency to favor the underdog. The problem with this is, playing the victim comes at a very high price that is often too burdensome to bear. Hell, it can sometimes be fatal. So, why play the victim when you're the only one who actually has the power to fix your own situation?

By blaming others, you give your power to them. Do you really want to give other people power over your life?

Probably not! If someone, or a situation is to blame, then in your mind, they are the ones responsible for fixing it, since they are the ones who caused the problem in the first place. They broke your life, so they must have the solution to fix it, right? **WRONG!**

Do you see how this renders you powerless? You can't control people or situations. Since you can't control people or situations, you shouldn't expect them to have the solution to your problem. Key word "your" problem. Give up the thought, it's just not going to happen. Everyone has problems of their own. Truly, they can't be concerned with your problems. When you point one finger at people, three more are pointing back at you. Literally, by you. That's right. You point one at them and three at yourself. An important reason to give up the blame game.

Having this kind of mindset means you're still struggling with your past. Staying mentally in your past causes you to keep re-enacting certain situations in your mind, engaging in all sorts of woulda, coulda, and shoulda, scenarios. Have you ever heard the phrase 'stuck like chuck?' LOL, I know it's 'ole school' but you know what it is. The more you dwell on your past, moving forward toward any real success becomes nearly impossible. Do you want to be mentally stuck in a place where you can't change anything? Of course, you don't.

Mental Roadblock #2: It's Impossible to Change

Change is not only possible; it's inevitable. In fact, it's the only constant that we can depend on, just look how the year 2020 played out. Having this toxic mindset is not as definite as you may think. People who suffer with this mindset actually put it in many different ways depending on the situations. However, they phrase it, this mentality still leads to a revolving door of losses that land you back at square one.

You either say that something is outright impossible; things are just not right; or you're waiting for the perfect set of circumstances. Either way, the more you think like this, the more you prevent yourself from taking action. "The timing is not right" is something else you may have told yourself. Or, maybe you convinced yourself that you don't have enough resources to get started in that opportunity. Whatever is keeping your heels from hitting the runway, all excuses lead to the same place; the land of stagnation or procrastination. You've given yourself all the justification you need to continue doing things exactly the same way you've always done them. You realize that change is necessary to improve your life. Typically, that's not the problem, neither is willingness the issue. Instead, you believe that it's impossible for you to change because of your past and because you have so many things going on in your life. Straight up Queen banish this idea!

Listen, you must understand that real change is actually possible when you chose it. Make the decision to change your mindset, then commit to taking the necessary steps to make it happen for yourself. PERIOD. No ifs, ands, or buts about it. Just get it done! Quit waiting for the right set of circumstances, the right time, the right resources, or the right people to come along. Hell, what if they never come?

Once you believe real change is possible, circumstances will present themselves because your mind is now opened to start receiving them. If you sit around waiting on the perfect circumstances, chances are, they'll never come. By believing that your mission is impossible, you actually jeopardize any positive change that you're seeking.

Mental Roadblock #3: Focusing on the Past

A lot of people who are striving for success end up sabotaging themselves because they believe that their past keeps them from achieving any great success in the future. They believe they've messed up so much, or so severely in the past that any future victories are really not within their reach. Instead of going for the gold medal, they're only aiming for the silver or bronze, and that's if they plan on placing at all. Most are just going through the motions. They've thrown in the towel in the first round of the fight.

Another perspective is thinking that you have to start with a completely clean slate in order to make any real changes in your life. In other words, you believe that you must be perfect. *News flash:* There are no perfect people on this planet. Mistakes made in the past don't hold a lot of weight on your future, unless you allow them to. Don't focus on your past, concentrate on your future. Stop letting your past discourage you from giving it your best shot now! Your past does not define who you are today, or who you could be tomorrow. You may have failed over and over again in the past, but that does not prevent you from getting it right, now. Actually, when you learn from your failures, you can use those lessons to build upon so that you achieve success this time around.

Mental Roadblock #4: Believing That You Can't Be Helped

This mindset believes that you are beyond help. That you are the only one who can fix things in your life. And although that may be true to a point, understand that no one makes it to the top by themselves. Unfortunately, you believe that the only person you must rely on is yourself and you have to figure it all out on your own. Thankfully, this isn't true.

Let's be clear, there's nothing new under the sun. The same issues you're dealing with, other people have dealt with before too. Although their circumstances may have been a little different, these people may be a good resource for you, if you ask. Listen, a closed mouth never gets fed. If you know a person who has weathered many storms, reach out to them personally and setup a meeting, or some type of mentorship situation. If they're influencers, maybe they can be a resource to you through their articles, blogs, books or even video courses they have created. No matter how you get the help, put your ego aside and get it! It really is that simple. In 2021, your situation is not unique. Whatever challenges you're facing; others have faced them and have overcome them. Allow their experiences to inspire you.

Another symptom of this toxic mindset is the belief that others won't be willing to help you. You've fooled yourself into believing that they won't give out their "secret sauce," or maybe they don't want any more competition. What does this sound like to you? More excuses, right? Right. In reality, you simply won't know for sure if people will help you, until you ask. Remember, a closed mouth never gets fed. Keeping your mouth closed won't get you what you need. Opening your mouth and asking for what you need increases your chances of receiving it.

And remember, just because one person is stingy with information, it doesn't mean that all people will be. Keep asking and don't give up. Keep asking until someone says "yes". Believe me, someone will help.

Mental Roadblock #5: Feeling Unworthy

Feeling like you don't deserve happiness, love, or success. This mindset is a tremendously toxic one. You won't find many people willing to admit they have this belief. However, deep down, most people believe this about themselves. After failing multiple times, some people adopt the belief that they don't deserve success. They end up defining themselves based on their own disappointments. In other ways, they have personalized their failures and setbacks by internalizing them in the worst way.

People who suffer with this mindset, believe that failure is not just something that happens when they strive for greatness or strive to achieve their goals, instead failure is some sort of cosmic punishment reserved exclusively for them. It's pretty sad, but they really believe that failure is some sort of fate of the "gods". They believe it burns deep and there's nothing that can be done to escape this fate. They believe it's permanent. This is a Greek myth and is also relentless in condemnation. Talk about incapacitating, geez…

This mindset also comes from having a traumatic background. Trauma yields self-esteem so low that those who suffer with it believe they aren't worthy of anything good. They believe and even put the needs of others before their own. They look at themselves as an emotional doormat. Is this you? Hasn't this gotten old? *Mental note*: you're the only person who gets to decide if YOU deserve success, no one else. You call the shots. You dictate the terms. No-one is in the position to judge you and say, "You don't deserve success." Listen, start claiming and declaring success in your life, and do it with the attitude that you know you deserve it. Because you do!

Mental Roadblock #6: Having a Perfection Complex

Just as toxic as believing you're unworthy, is having the mindset that you're perfect the way you are, and that you don't have to change. You believe that you're the smartest person in the room; definitely the best looking. Heck, you even believe that you're all that and a bag of chips.

While it's good to have a positive self-image and a healthy self-esteem, don't be fooled into believing that you don't need help or that you don't need to make any changes. Mental note: change is required on your road to success. This means letting go of whatever inflated impressions of yourself you may be holding on to. Take on the perspective that there's always room for improvement. Understand that this doesn't make you any less important, nor does it mean you're defeated.

Mental Roadblock #7: Promising & Then Procrastinating

This mindset believes that "there's always tomorrow." Why are you playing this game with yourself? Always making promises to change but then never changing. Always putting things off until tomorrow. You know that tomorrow isn't promised to anyone, yet you play this game like it is. Mental note: tomorrow never comes for some people and it might not come for you either.

Stop making promises to change, even saying it out loud but then turning around and saying, "I'll do it tomorrow". If you're waiting on the right time, understand that the time will never be right. You and I both know that something will always 'come up' that seems like a higher priority, and it will prevent you from making the required changes. Stop promising and then procrastinating. Make a commitment, stick to it, and then take action!

By starting today, you learn lessons you need to learn sooner rather than later. Since you're going through this process anyway at some point in the future, why not do it now and get it over with?

Mental Roadblock #8: Money Isn't Everything

Interestingly, the very people who say that money isn't everything are usually the same people who want a lot of money. You know, the ones always trying to keep up with the Joneses. The same applies to people who have tried and failed to achieve great success in their lives. You recognize them when they say things like "it wasn't worth the trouble anyway" or "I'm focused on something else; there are more important things in life." *Mental note*: These are the comments made by angry people who have not achieved something they wanted. If money and success aren't valuable to you, then why were you pursuing them? Why are you treating them like a consolation prize? This mindset has cost people millions. Stop playing this game with yourself. It's just another excuse not to improve. You know you want the gold, so go for it! Stop making excuses and do the work!

Mental Roadblock #9: Success is Not Worth The Trouble

This mindset is very complex and yet toxic because it has a lot of moving parts. Some people end with this conclusion because they believe they don't want to betray their own personal values. You may have heard people say; "I just want to protect my soul." "I don't want to lose my soul or my identity chasing success." Or what about this one, "I'm just keeping it real". Chances are, you probably said this yourself. Regardless of how you phrase it, these are all excuses! When you get rid of this way of thinking, success can become part of your identity and core values.

Maybe you got burnt in the past or you've been deeply disappointed. Whatever it was, you must not use the past as an excuse to not take action today. Success is worth it because it develops you. You become a better version of yourself. It teaches you the value of sacrifice. It enables you to gain a sense of purpose in your life. Living a life of purpose is one of the most rewarding gifts you can ever give to yourself. When you take action every day toward your goals, it's empowering to realize that the steps you take leads to somewhere phenomenal.

Mental Roadblock #10: If I Win Someone Else Will Lose

This way of thinking stems from having a zero-sum mindset. A what? A zero-sum mindset is an assumption that for one person to win, the other person must lose. You should know that there is no giant pie of success in the world. Your slice getting bigger doesn't mean that someone else's piece of the pie gets smaller. We all want different things, and there's enough out here for everyone to win!

There are a lot of opportunities that come and go all the time. When you strive for success and excellence, you inspire others to do the same. Don't go on thinking that people will envy you. Envious people operate with a zero-sum mindset. Your success doesn't mean you cause someone else's piece of the pie to shrink.

When you choose to inspire others, you're in a sense sharing success because people can be motivated to achieve success for themselves. This theory is the exact opposite of the shrinking pie theory. If anything, you increase the pie's size and ensure more slices for others who want it.

Chapter Two

BELIEVE THAT YOU CAN CHANGE & YOU WILL

First and foremost, pay close attention to your assumptions; they are ESSENTIAL and have a tremendous impact on your life. An assumption is what you believe about your life, capabilities, identity, where you are in the world, and your rightful place. These assumptions are CHOICES.

You choose to interpret reality; this is not permanent. No rule says that you must interpret reality in only one particular way. However, you must learn to control your assumptions. They might not be top of mind and may not be obvious, but you can control them when they come to you. *Mental note:* Change is the only constant in life.

Believe it or not, you're already changing just by reading this book. As you get older, some of what you believe about yourself could be a result of the number of trips you've taken around the sun. They say we get better with age, just like fine wine. Regardless, changes are part of who you are. Change happens on two fundamental levels: you can change from within and change outward. You must believe that your ability to change is the key to rewriting your mental script. If you don't think change is necessary, it will be almost impossible for you to implement a success mindset. Change is not optional, nor is it negotiable. Change is inevitable.

To help strengthen your belief muscles. Think about some examples from your past where you had to change, and you did. Using the ever-popular losing weight analogy, at first, you weren't excited about working out. You knew you had gained weight and that changes would be necessary for you to lose it. One of which is becoming physically active again. After a couple of weeks, you finally get to the point where you are working out consistently. Look for examples like this. It doesn't have to be extreme or dramatic. Regardless, I'm sure you have at least three examples from your past where you had to make a change, and you did.

Next, analyze what happened. Pay attention to what prompted the change. Why did you believe you had to change? What circumstances were present? What was your situation? What was the straw that broke the camel's back? Now, focus on how you were before and how you were after the change. Look at the difference. Then ask, "What do these experiences teach me about myself? Are you the person who waits until the last minute, and disaster is only lurking around the corner for you to make a bold move?" Maybe you finally got a job because you were about to get kicked out of your place; perhaps your company announced a significant layoff but offered a test to people who wanted to stay on. Whatever your specific experience was, pay attention to how you responded. Did you wait until you were backed into a corner with no place to go before you were forced to make a decision? Or did you want specific changes all along, and situations just pushed you to make the decision? Are you a reactive or proactive person? Either you're reactive, which means you are motivated primarily by the fear of loss, or proactive, which means you are motivated by the possibility of gain. If you are a reactive person, dwell on what you can lose in your life if you don't push yourself to change. If you are proactive, focus on how much better your life would be realizing your dreams if only you allowed yourself to change.

Chapter Three

FAILURE IS NOT TO BE FEARED – BUT EMBRACED

I t's imperative to make sure you understand that setbacks happen. Not just to you, but everyone experiences them. People fail all the time. When it happens, your failure may seem devastating and often feels humiliating, but failure is part of life in the big scheme of things. Instead of fearing or wishing failure away or continuously asking yourself, "why me?" expect it, and then embrace it.

According to Thomas Stanley's book "The Millionaire Next Door," the average millionaire has gone bankrupt more than three times. Now, let that marinate for a second. Do you know how crushing a bankruptcy is? It's personally humiliating. Sure, the stigma has worn off bankruptcy, but it's still a major personal setback. Yet, it didn't hold these millionaires back. They peaked, they crashed and burned, then they got back up. So, stop fearing failure. Instead, focus on what comes next. Failure doesn't have to stop there, and it's doesn't have to be the end of your journey. Dispel the belief that if you're expecting failure, you want it to happen, or you wish for it to happen. No. These are two separate things.

When you expect failure, you understand that the likelihood of failure is always there. By anticipating that the worst can happen, you then permit yourself to respond so that you allow yourself to bounce back.

Learn How to Measure Success

Often, we think that we've failed and that we just crashed and burned. But what happened was, we measured our success wrong. For example, if you start a new business and you've projected a return on your investment in five years, it would be absurd for you to expect a return on your investment in the first year. If this is how you're thinking, you'll only beat yourself up needlessly. Measure your success correctly and in the appropriate way. It may well turn out that you did not fail at all; you're merely waiting. Exercise patience but keep going. Head up - heart strong.

Fail Quickly – But Fail Forward

Along with measuring your success correctly, another way to prepare for failure is to decide to fail quickly and fail forward. Yup, you heard me right, fail quickly but fail forward (always moving toward the prize). I know this sounds somewhat crazy, but a lot of successful people do this. They know that achieving success involves a lot of trial and error, so they experiment a lot. It's like throwing spaghetti against the wall—eventually, one-piece sticks. So be quick about throwing the spaghetti against the wall and getting it to bounce off. When you do this, you're navigating your way to success. The secret is to fail quickly and inexpensively. It must not leave any scars and it must not bankrupt you.

Controlling Your Emotions

Do not let your setbacks define you. Learn how to control your emotions. Losing control of them is the number one reason why some people fail. You see, just because your business venture did not give you the win you expected doesn't mean that you've failed and should quit. It could mean that you need to experiment a little more or even pivot and go in a different direction. Regardless, keep going. Keep moving forward!

If you somehow think a setback is the end of the world or that you're a loser, you've allowed the setback to define you. Setbacks are hard pills to swallow and can hurt. Sometimes it's hard to move on. So, when the next opportunity presents itself to you, you find yourself hesitating, or you ignore it altogether.

Yes, setbacks can evoke a strong emotional response, but they don't have to define you. Experiencing a setback doesn't mean that you're a screw-up and won't ever get it together, either. So, what should you do? Keep going.

Journal Daily

Ever heard the saying, 'You don't know where you're going unless you know where you've been?' When you keep a journal of your efforts, you're doing yourself a considerable favor as it relates to achieving ultimate success. When a failure does knock at your door, you can look in your journal to figure out why things went awry. A journal allows you to clearly identify what you did before, during, and after the setback. Equipped with this information, you can choose to do things differently. You start to connect the dots. Yes, you can see patterns and conduct experiments to see if you get better results. Throughout all of this, focus on your end goal.

So, how important is it to keep a journal? Well, people looking to lose weight reported receiving better results when they journaled what they ate. Even eating the same food types as before and in the exact amounts, these test participants still experienced weight loss. Likewise, the same principle applies when it comes to success. Get a journal. Write it down.

The Key to Success In Spite of Failure

Failure is a part of life. Embrace it. Prepare for it. *Mental note:* when you persevere, success usually follows.

According to a research study published by Professor Angela Duckworth, perseverance is the secret of success. It's not about being the smartest person in the room. It's not about being the most dedicated and motivated person. Instead, it's all about the ability to get knocked down but still, get back up and keep pushing forward. Donnie McClurkin said in his song, "We Fall Down, But We Get Up."

Regardless of how many times you get knocked down, get turned around, or get postponed, keep pushing forward until you get what you were going after. That's right. Keep pushing to the end. Perseverance is a choice. It is the ultimate remedy to a setback.

Chapter Four

SETTING GOALS EMPOWERS YOU TO ACHIEVE THEM

Most people are struggling to attain success. The problem for some is they view goals as afterthoughts. Some believe that goals are irrelevant, even permanent, so they chose not to set goals at all. Then you have those who would prefer to follow their passion, flying by the seat of their pants hoping that eventually, they'll achieve success. At least, this is what they think. Talk about getting it wrong. SMH.

Goals are like directions on a map. You write them down and follow them until you reach your destination. Having this map allows you to see what happens before, during, and after achieving your goal. To accomplish your goals, you must create sub-goals. These are mini-goals that lead to your ultimate goal. Mini-goals are more attainable and allow you to understand what process is needed, the decisions required, and the results you have to produce along the way.

You get to see the potential dead ends, bumps in the road, and detours. Sub-goals can give you milestones to which you can then add timelines to motivate you to take action because you can see that you'll reach part of your success journey by a particular time.

What's Easy to Do – Is Easy Not to Do

Goals are relatively easy to describe and reasonably easy to understand. However, most people still don't achieve them. Why not? Saying you want to do something is easier said than done; putting your money where your mouth is something altogether different because most people view goals as something, they should work for instead of being something they plan to achieve. They view them as being optional.

Some believe that you should pursue goals when the time is right or when they think they have the right circumstances or resources. Most of the time, there's no sense of urgency, and they don't put themselves in a do or die situation. Given most people's mindsets about goals, it would be safe to say they act like they're some fantasy "To-Do List." Which is a far cry from how successful people view goals.

Successful People Are Defined by Their Goals

Successful people view goals in a completely different way. They structure their goals first around their passions. For example, you are passionate about modeling for a living, so your goal is to become a professional model. Now transform that goal and link it to your core passions. When you work towards these goals, you confirm your personal beliefs. You feel that you are expressing your real personality.

Best of all, tapping into your core skills will motivate you. There's an upward spiral that occurs when you work towards your goals: the more you achieve, the more confident and competent you become, the more inspired you become, and the more action you take. This vortex or spiral can either go up or down.

When it goes up, you experience a tremendous amount of pride. Achieving your goals gives you a "bossed-up" sense of achievement. You get the idea that this is what you're supposed to be doing. When you operate from this perspective, goals are no longer things that you should be doing. Instead, you realize that they are things that you were born to do. Something that you must do. See the contrast?

Your Goals Should Move You to Take Action

If your goals don't motivate and push you to expect more from yourself, you need to change them. Understand that your goals are not permanent. They are simply tools that can be modified, so treat them that way.

First, you must redefine your goals. Determine what's truly at stake. Is it a matter of getting certain things done by a particular date, or is it a matter of you leveling up? Bringing your A game.

Change your goals by asking yourself, "What will success mean to and for me?" How does achieving this goal make me a better person?" When you change your goals, you can refocus. Looking at your goals as directly linked to the values you've set for yourself can motivate you even more. Remember, this is not just one set of things that you do daily. It's what gives your life purpose to move forward every day.

Let's Review

Goals must do the following; otherwise, they must be redefined, changed, and refocused. First, they must motivate you. Understanding your "why" helps you to accomplish them. That's right. You must understand your "why." Why did you set these goals? Why must you achieve these goals? What is your reasoning behind what you're doing? When you actively work toward your goals, you gain a sense of purpose.

There's a pep in your step. You're no longer flying by the seat of your pants. Instead, you're doing something that has a real meaning behind it; there is purpose.

Next, your goals must direct you to take action because you have an objective. Goals must, at the very least, guide you so that you're focused on how and what to do. Finally, you need to break down your goals because when you list them as singular items, they appear harder to accomplish. When you break down your goals into smaller sub-goals, they seem more attainable. Sub-goals and a daily to-do list only scratch the surface. Repetition is the key.

Being able to follow through day after day, week after week, month after month, and year after year. Make sure that your goals and daily "things to do list" are scalable. You must be able to scale them up, so improvements on one level lead to more comfortable and more defined improvements on other levels. Along with being scalable, you must measure your goals to be sure that you're achieving them. My advice set the quality of standards for you to measure them.

Finally, when you're setting your goals, you must have an emotional connection to them. Associate your goals with a sense of accomplishment, destiny, success, and purpose. If you have no emotional connection with your goals, they aren't goals at all; they're just words on paper. You know, "things" that you should be doing at some point but never do. Remember, people believe they don't have the time, energy, or attention for things they should be doing. Instead, they focus on the things they MUST be doing. Accomplishing your goals must be a do or die situation. You must work on them daily and as though your life depended on it.

Your Actions Become Habits

The good news is, the more you achieve your sub-goals, the more your actions become habits. Success is a habit, not something that happens by chance but something that happens by change. Remember, success is something that you attract. It's looking for a great place to live. As you work toward your goals, keep in mind that what you are looking for is also looking for you.

Chapter Five

YOUR GOALS DON'T CARE ABOUT EXCUSES, JUST RESULTS

uccess is an act of displaying FAITH. No, seriously. When you believe in something, you take action. You don't wait around for a random chance to deliver results, nor do you wait for things to 'feel right' or miraculously 'fall into place.' You and I both know; they seldom fall into place. The last time I checked, most people don't just get rich. They plan to get rich. They activate their plans by taking action! The secret here is to believe in your goals and then take action, requiring commitment, persistence, and dedication.

Taking action is more than making one attempt and then hoping for the best. Instead, it requires you to take consistent action, day after day, week after week. You see, your goals don't care about how you feel or the drama you have going on. Your goals don't care about fantasies, *only results*. What's going on in your life or what people are saying about you doesn't matter. None of that matters. What you do matters. Ultimately, this takes faith. Real faith takes action over and over again.

Faith believes in the things hoped for. It's the kind of faith you must have as you take steps to accomplish your goals. You will experience many challenges, and there will be one setback after another. Prepare for them, but don't give up. Keep in mind that a setback is a setup for a comeback! Ha!

Remember, if you can't get in through the front door, take the side door. If that doesn't work, go around back, and if you can't get through that door, fuck it, create one yourself. Keep in mind that success is not something you accomplish alone; seek help from experienced professionals who have already been where you're attempting to go.

Celebrate Your Accomplishments – Even the Small Wins!

Did you know that most successful people celebrate the mere fact that they took action? They take a step back to acknowledge what they are doing at that particular time. They are fully aware that they are taking action and how that action will lead to a specific goal. It's called celebrating the small wins. My advice, you should do the same because it allows you to move past the hoping, wishing, or fantasizing stage. You wouldn't believe how many people spend their days daydreaming about the kind of lives they could be living "if" only.

Are you guilty of being this type of daydreamer? Hoping and wishing that somehow, or some way, the best things in life will just happen to you. We've all been there. Lots of people waste a tremendous amount of time daydreaming and fantasizing. Wake up! Things won't get better by chance; they get better by change.

Another truth, people daydream because it gives them an emotional release. Regardless of how frustrating their current situation may be, when they imagine themselves in the future where they are free of their current problems, it's an emotional rush. The problem is, you can get addicted to this emotional rush and stay stuck in your situation.

Sadly, the more people daydream, the worse off they are. Why? Because they aren't taking the actual steps (action) needed to make those dreams come true. Remind yourself that you're not just waiting for things to happen; you're making them happen.

Celebrating your ability to shape your reality and establish your destiny doesn't have to be large or expensive. Still, it can be the carrot you dangle in front of yourself when you need that extra motivation.

The More Action You Take, the More Effective You Become

As you become aware that you're practicing your ability to take action, it starts a chain reaction. You become more proactive. You develop the habit of working towards your goals. Significantly, you learn how to fail faster, which leads to faster learning.

This activity then increases your chance of meeting new opportunities, which in turn leads to the possibility of greater success. It's all tied in together, and all it takes is the commitment to take action. Remember, Success is an act of faith.

Chapter Six

MAKE A DECISION & STICK TO IT

You can't be indecisive and become truly successful. Fortunately, that's not how it happens. Why? While opportunities appear quickly, but they also disappear just as quickly. Don't waste time analyzing what could be, going back and forth with yourself about what could happen, and other possible eventualities. Weigh out your choices, figure out what's at stake, then make a decision. You must <u>DECIDE</u> what you're going to do and then do it.

Analysis Paralysis – An Excuse to Not Take Action

Do you look for more data before deciding on a problem or an opportunity? Maybe you believe that somehow if you get enough information, you'll make the right decision. Really what's happening here is, you're finding yet another excuse not to take action. Trust and believe that there's never a time when knowing "everything" will make all the risks disappear. Time and opportunity wait for no-one. Make a decision.

I hate to be the bearer of bad news, but there's no 'magic bullet' piece of information that will be like a beacon shining through the heavens. Sorry, not sorry, nothing you come across will guarantee that your next move will be your best move. If only it were that simple. The key is not to freak yourself out when deciding.

Set a deadline, but not too close that you end up intimidating yourself. On the other hand, it shouldn't be too far away either. Setting it too far in advance gives you the impression that you have time. Then, when it's time to pull the trigger, you're not prepared. Bottom line pick the correct date.

Action Speaks Louder Than Words

When you decide, you're not just going through some mental exercise; you commit to walking the talk. You haven't decided if you've not taken action, and there are no risks.

You know that you've decided when you're ready to look uncertainty right in the face and take it head-on. It means that you're prepared to say 'no' to things that distract you from reaching your goals. It won't be easy. However, when you commit, you prepare for the 'what ifs' that can and will happen. At the very least, you're going in with the mindset to improvise, innovate, or negotiate. I'm not saying you should expect things to be smooth sailing. You're making a commitment to keep going no matter what.

Knowing When to Pivot

Yes. This part. While making a decision means you're going to take action and commit to the end goal, it also means knowing when to pivot. There has to be a limit if things are not panning out, knowing when to pivot will prevent you from continuing down a path that could rob you of opportunity costs. Opportunity costs represent the potential benefits a business misses out on when choosing one alternative over another, which can be very expensive. You don't want to continue doing something with an eventual payoff of $2 when you could have pivoted and chosen a different direction that pays you $200. *Mental note*: Know when to pivot and then do it.

Key Points to Remember

When you commit, it speaks volumes about your character. What kind of person do you want to be? What kind of person do you picture yourself becoming? Buyer beware: This image you created for yourself is in danger if you don't know how to commit. If you're indecisive, continually changing your mind, or quitting too quickly, you'll never develop the character you would like for yourself. So, make it personal.

People may think you're all that and a bag of chips, but their compliments go in one ear and out of the other because deep down, you know you can't commit. You feel a lack of accomplishment despite what everybody else sees in you. Make it personal. There has to be some "fire" from within that makes you stick to your commitment.

Chapter Seven

REMAIN A STUDENT – DON'T BE LAZY IN LEARNING

Even if you've done some significant research about your goals, it doesn't mean that you know everything. There is always room for improvement. There will always be things that you don't know.

However, the more living you do, the older you get, the more likely you are to make assumptions. Since you've been around the block a few times, you think you've done and seen it all. That would be a mistake. No-one knows everything. Do you remember what the old folks use to say about assuming? Yes. That part.

Assumptions undermine actual learning and can keep you from looking at your problem through a set of clear lens and with an open mind. Instead, you believe that if you see specific patterns, you'll be able to use solutions that worked in the past. BIG mistake! Don't make it. Remember, nothing stays the same, especially in this day and age. Remain a student, don't be lazy in learning.

Cultivate a Growth Mindset

When you develop a growth mindset, you go into each situation, understanding that there will be a learning curve. Remember that even though you may have gone down this road in the past, you haven't done this exact project before, so things will be different.

When there are limitations to your knowledge, reach out for help. This allows you to grow. Don't be afraid to ask for help. People will help you and give you access to resources that you'll need. How does it work? When operating with a growth mindset, you first focus on your core competencies (skills). We all have skills that we're good at or have mastered. Find yours. Once you've identified them, work outward from there.

Here's how I do it. I look at my goals, then break them down based on my core competencies. I then make a list of the things that I know like the back of my hand, and then everything else follows. These are called non-core skills, which could be delegated to someone else, outsourced, postponed, or flat out ignored. It depends on their importance and their effects on my ultimate goal and how pressing they are.

Regardless, if they fall outside of my core competencies, I do not hesitate to delegate, outsource, postpone, or ignore them.

Always stay within your wheelhouse; this increases your mastery over your project. You focus on what's essential and leave the other stuff on your list to specialists who are experienced in those areas. *This is a BOSS move!*

Chapter Eight

EVERY PROBLEM HAS A SOLUTION – REMAIN CONFIDENT YOU'LL FIND IT

People are overwhelmed with problems not because they lack intelligence or are unlucky. In most cases, they are not prepared. Without having a system in place, it comes as no surprise that they struggle when a setback occurs.

Now, I'm not saying that you have to know precisely what will happen in the future. That's not possible. It also doesn't mean that you have to anticipate every potential setback. Instead, implementing the following system helps you prepare for the unexpected, so you're not caught off guard.

Recognize

The first thing you must do is recognize the opportunity shown in the problem that needs solving. They say that opportunities often come disguised as challenges. Find the opportunity in this situation. Then ask yourself: What can I learn from this situation? How can this situation make me better?

No matter how small, use the lesson as motivation or inspiration to come up with a solution. If anything, you'll learn something new, solve the problem and come out on top, instead of allowing it to overtake or frustrate you.

Enhance

Now that you've come up with a solution take it for a spin. That's right; give it a test run. Is it efficient? Figure out ways to get faster results. Test multiple times until you are satisfied that you've found the best solution for that particular situation.

Dominate

Once you've found the solution, it's time to master the problem. You're a BOSS. Right. Now wear the crown. You not only want the solution for your immediate issue, but you want a solution that goes well into the future and helps to solve a variety of problems. Either way, rise to the occasion and stare the problem right in the eyes and do what Bosses do; *WE DOMINATE!*

Scale Up

Now that you've dominated the problem by coming up with an enhanced solution use it often. Yup, scale-up. Come up with another version of this solution. For instance, if you've always had trouble meeting deadlines, you can enhance or adjust the solution to help you now meet deadlines. You then dominate or control the situation by setting up a system, so you're always on time. You can then apply this solution to other areas of your life, like personal relationships. It means that you're never late for another anniversary or any other important event moving forward.

Cutting Your Losses

While learning how to recognize, enhance, dominate, and scale up is important, certain problems are just impossible. If you find yourself in this situation, or if you believe that you've hit a wall that is impossible to breach, you must pivot and cut your losses.

Chapter Nine

SUCCESSFUL PEOPLE ARE COGNIZANT OF THE RISK AND TAKE THEM AWAY

As an investor, I'm often asked, "How do you avoid risks?" My answer is always the same, "you don't." If you're looking for a high reward, you must take on more risks. Successful people know that risks are inevitable. Consequently, they take assessed risks because they understand the greater the risk, the greater the reward.

Unfortunately, imposters (people trying to copy successful people) often miss the mark. They take shots in the dark with hopes of hitting something and dream of getting lucky. It's a gamble, not a calculated risk for them. Being a copycat is not a boss move, even when you're copying the right cat! Yup. That part.

Risk-taking only happens when you understand what you stand to gain and lose. When gambling, you focus on the odds; it's generally where your attention lies. When you take calculated risks, you look at what's currently happening, what could happen, and only then do you make strategic decisions.

The good news is, the more you understand the move you're about to make, the lower your risks. You can't entirely make risks go away, but you can manage them. Successful people always find ways to take on more risks while managing them. They run to, not away from risks, and they almost always have a Plan B.

It's like having an insurance policy because they've been in situations often enough to know that something will happen that's out of their control. They need to be able to figure out a way around the pitfalls to keep moving. Eventually, we keep repeating this over and over again to achieve impressive results and control the risk.

Chapter Ten

IMPLEMENTING A SUCCESS MINDSET

Congrats! You've reached the end of this book. And as powerful and empowering as the information shared may seem, nothing changes in your life until you take action. Please don't treat this information like it's "motivational." That's not going to help you. Motivation can only take you so far. You must implement what you've learned for them to make a difference in your life. Tailor them to fit your needs. Once you've done this, here are some best practices to follow that will help improve your results.

Mindsets are Like Muscles – Use Them or Lose Them

When you implement these mindsets, please give them a test run before diving headfirst. Use these mindsets and challenge their legitimacy. Remember the first time you tried lifting weights? It started uncomfortably, but with repetition, the more your muscles got used to the pressure. You could lift heavier weights because you challenged your muscles by getting them use to the repetitive patterns. The same applies to mindsets.

It's not enough for you to use these mindsets once or even twice. The repetitive motion helps you form the habit of using them often. Thus, they become a part of you. Start using your muscles in different techniques. Scale up the challenge, then add resistance. You have to apply pressure, so your muscles get stronger and produce better results.

Start Now, Don't Wait

Tomorrow is promised to no-one, so start now! Don't wait. You don't have to do much, but you do have to start by taking action. Understand that the time and circumstances will never be just right. When are they ever just right? Exactly, never! So, don't make excuses and don't procrastinate. Redirect your energy and commit to getting started right now!

Every Setback is a Setup for a Comeback!

I think it was Les Brown who said, "A setback is a setup for a comeback!" Make no mistake; you're going to run into problems when you implement the success mindsets described in this book. For whatever reason, there will be a hurdle or two to jump over. No-one knows why; that's just life.

So, instead of feeling defeated or getting frustrated whenever you experience a setback, look at it as an opportunity to learn. Just remember to leave your emotions out of it and instead focus on the perception that this was expected. Although you may not have known precisely what problem was going to rear its ugly little head, you knew a curveball would be thrown. The good news is, you had your gloves on because you were ready for whatever. Remember, when you stay ready, you don't have to get ready.

When preparation meets opportunity, it equals success! Taking up this attitude or being in this frame of mind allows you to look at the setback as an opportunity to come back.

What could you have done differently? What should your attitude have been? How can you anticipate this problem and prevent it from happening in the future? Regardless, be ready to learn. One of the best attitudes to have when implementing these new mindsets is that of a student. When you're a student, you put yourself in the mindset for learning, so mistakes are not exactly the end of the world. Instead, you often laugh, figure it out, then you do it again and again until it's second nature.

Develop a System to Decrease Your Risk

Finally, you should develop a system and use it. In this book, I've discussed one way to deal with setbacks: to recognize, enhance, dominate, and scale. But you should come up with your own version, something that fits your current situation.

What I've given you in this book is a starting point that lays out a basic foundation. It's up to you to incorporate them into your life, so they produce the results you desire.

CONCLUSION

Thank you for reading this book. When you implement the ideas within it, they can change your life.

Please understand that the results that you get in life stem directly from your mindset.

Everything comes from your mindset (the way you think) because it determines how you understand the world. It also influences your emotional response to it.

Change your mindset; this changes your behavior, which changes your results. If you're not happy with your present situation, then the most powerful and effective way to change your situation would be to change your mindset.

I wish you massive success!

Cassondra Khadijah Adams

Founder of Khadijah Adams, LLC dba Girl Get That Money

Cassondra "Khadijah" Adams is a mother of 4 amazing adult sons and a grandmother of 10 beautiful grandchildren. She is originally from Sugar Land, Texas. Khadijah started her first business while raising her children as a single mother. In 1997 she realized that she was allergic to bosses and decided to try her hand at entrepreneurship. Khadijah founded Parker Paralegal Services, Inc. dba Certified Signing Services where sales reached over a million dollars annually. After 10 successful years in business, the real estate industry took a turn for the worse, and Khadijah was forced to close her doors in 2007.

In 2008, she took her last $6,000 and invested it all into a computer retail business. Three months after opening, the company had sold over $120,000 worth of computers. The company later expanded by opening 2 more retail storefronts and by launching an online e-commerce store, all of which were successful and collectively generated a high sixfigure income.

In 2014, when the state of Colorado legalized cannabis for recreational consumption, Ms. Adams sold her business and all of her worldly possessions with the exception of her car, cell phone, clothes, and computer, and moved to Colorado to get in on the "Green Rush". By late November of that year, Khadijah and a business partner formed Marijuana Investment & Private Retreat aka MIPR Holdings, LLC, a cannabis consulting, and investor relations firm located in Aurora, Colorado where she served as the founder and senior managing partner for 3-1/2 years.

In June 2017, MIPR, LLC, and MIPR Holdings, LLC was later acquired by C. E. Hutton, LLC, a business development and management firm in Denver, Colorado where Ms. Adams currently sits on the Board of Managers as the Vice President. She is also the Founder of The GreenStreet Academy, an online educational platform that teaches the basics of investing in the marijuana industry, and the co-author of The Minority Report, annual marketing analysis of Minority-owned companies in the cannabis and hemp industries. On May 1, 2020, Ms. Adams launched Khadijah Adams, LLC dba Girl Get That Money, a business empowerment coaching and consultancy movement focused on women in business and women aspiring to be in business.

Ms. Adams is a motivational and public speaker. She sits on the Advisory Board of The Color of Cannabis (TCC) 2020-2021, and is the Chair of the Diversity, Equity, and Inclusion Committee (DEIC) of the National Cannabis Industry Association (NCIA) 2020-2021.

www.ingramcontent.com/pod-product-compliance
Lightning Source LLC
Chambersburg PA
CBHW070057100426
42740CB00013B/2867